FABLES

D1300047

THE NEW ADVENTURES OF JACK AND JACK

DUE

JACK of FABLES

THE NEW ADVENTURES of JACK AND JACK

BILL WILLINGHAM
MATTHEW STURGES
CHRIS ROBERSON
WRITERS

RUSS BRAUN ✳ **TONY AKINS**
PENCILLERS

JOSÉ MARZÁN, JR. ✳ **ANDREW PEPOY**
TONY AKINS ✳ **RUSS BRAUN**
INKERS

DANIEL VOZZO
COLORIST

TODD KLEIN
LETTERER

BRIAN BOLLAND
ORIGINAL SERIES COVERS

Jack of Fables created by **BILL WILLINGHAM**

Cover illustration by BRIAN BOLLAND
Logo design by JAMES JEAN

JACK OF FABLES: THE NEW ADVENTURES OF JACK AND JACK

Published by DC Comics. Cover and compilation Copyright © 2010 DC Comics.
All Rights Reserved. Originally published in single magazine form as JACK OF FABLES 36-40.
Copyright © 2009, 2010 Bill Willingham and DC Comics. All Rights Reserved. All characters,
their distinctive likenesses and related elements featured in this publication are trademarks of
Bill Willingham. VERTIGO is a trademark of DC Comics. The stories, characters and incidents
featured in this publication are entirely fictional. DC Comics does not read or accept unsolicited
submissions of ideas, stories or artwork.

DC Comics, 1700 Broadway, New York, NY 10019
A Warner Bros. Entertainment Company.
Printed in the USA. First Printing.
ISBN: 978-1-4012-2712-8

SUSTAINABLE
FORESTRY
INITIATIVE

Certified Fiber Sourcing
www.sfiprogram.org

Fiber used in this product line meets the
sourcing requirements of the SFI program.
www.sfiprogram.org PWC-SFICOC-260

TABLE OF CONTENTS

Dramatis Personae

Jack

Also known as Little Jack Horner, Jack B. Nimble, Jack the Giant Killer and countless other aliases, our hero Jack of the Tales embodies the archetype of the lovable rogue (minus, according to many, the lovability).

Gary, the Pathetic Fallacy

A timid, impressionable and warm-hearted fellow who used to be one of the most powerful beings on the planet.

Jack Frost

The son of Jack Horner and Lumi, the Snow Queen, now grown up and looking for a direction in life.

Robin Page

One of the three Page Sisters, former chief librarians and enforcers for the now-defunct Fable prison known as the Golden Boughs Retirement Village.

Babe

A blue ox given to flights of fancy.

"WHO KNEW THAT MUSLIMS WOULD TAKE OFFENSE TO A
COMBINATION BROTHEL AND GAMBLING HOUSE?"

ANCHORAGE, ALASKA.

IT IS *COLD*, JACK.

IS IT? I DON'T TEND TO NOTICE.

TRUST ME, IT'S COLD.

CAN'T WE GO SOMEWHERE WARMER?

SURE, WHY NOT? WHERE'D YOU HAVE IN MIND, GARY? WE COULD GO CHECK OUT THE DESERTS, SEE WHERE I HELPED *LAWRENCE* CONQUER ARABIA.

OF COURSE, IT CAN GET A BIT SANDY OUT THERE.

I DON'T LIKE THE SAND. IT GETS IN MY BATHING SUIT AREAS.

IF YOU DON'T LIKE A DRY HEAT, WE COULD ALWAYS TRY THE STEAMY HEAT OF THE TROPICS. AFRICA SUIT YOUR FANCY? WE COULD CHECK IN WITH MY OLD FRIENDS FROM MY DAYS AS *LORD OF THE JUNGLE*.

WHEN WERE *YOU* LORD OF THE JUNGLE?

YOU MEAN WE'VE BEEN ON THE ROAD FOR ALL THIS TIME AND I'VE *NEVER* TOLD YOU ABOUT THAT?

9

IT WAS SOMEWHERE NEAR THE TAIL END OF THE NINETEENTH CENTURY, AND I WAS QUICKLY COMING TO THE CONCLUSION THAT AFRICA JUST WASN'T THE PLACE FOR ME.

I WAS STILL ON THE RUN FROM FABLETOWN'S FARM AFTER THAT OLD WEST OUTLAW BUSINESS, AND LOOKING FOR A PLACE TO HIDE OUT, AND MAYBE MAKE A LITTLE PROFIT IN THE MEANTIME.

I'D HAD TO LEAVE MOROCCO IN A HURRY, WITH A WARRANT OUT FOR MY ARREST. THE FACT THAT THE AUTHORITIES ISSUED THE WRIT ONLY AFTER TAKING MY BRIBES TO KEEP "JACK'S CAFÉ AMÉRICAIN" OPEN JUST ADDED INSULT TO INJURY.

WHO KNEW THAT MUSLIMS WOULD TAKE OFFENSE TO A COMBINATION BROTHEL AND GAMBLING HOUSE?

I WAS ON MY WAY TO SOUTH AFRICA, WHERE I FIGURED THERE WAS A FORTUNE TO BE MADE SWINDLING THE DIAMOND MINERS, WHEN I'D HAD THE BAD LUCK TO GET THROWN OVERBOARD IN NOTHING BUT MY SKIVVIES.

WHICH EXPLAINED WHY I FOUND MYSELF WASHED UP ON THE SHORES OF WEST AFRICA. HARDLY AN AUSPICIOUS BEGINNING TO MY NEXT EXCITING ADVENTURE.

JACK 'N' APES

GET YOUR PAWS OFF ME, YOU DAMNED DIRTY APE!

THERE'S NO NEED TO BE RUDE.

IT ISN'T AS IF HOT BATHS ARE EASY TO COME BY IN THE JUNGLE.

TELL ME ABOUT IT...

WAIT A MINUTE, YOU CAN TALK?!

FIRST HE INSULTS OUR HYGIENE, AND NOW OUR COMMUNICATION SKILLS ARE CALLED INTO QUESTION?

THAT'S HUMANS FOR YOU. NO MANNERS.

JUST WHAT KIND OF MONKEYS ARE YOU, ANYWAY?

DO YOU SEE A TAIL ON ME? WE'RE APES, SONNY-JIM.

IT'S JACK, ACTUALLY. JACK HORNER.

THE JACK HORNER?

FROM THE HOME-LANDS?

SOMETHING DIDN'T SMELL RIGHT. I MEAN, BESIDES THE STENCH OF UNWASHED APE.

HOW DO YOU KNOW ABOUT THE HOMELANDS?

UM, BECAUSE **WE** ARE FABLES, TOO?

DID YOU HIT YOUR **HEAD** FALLING OFF THAT BEANSTALK?

IF YOU'RE FABLES, WHAT ARE YOU DOING OFF THE FARM? I THOUGHT YOU **LESSER** SPECIES WERE ALL CONTAINED FOR YOUR OWN PROTECTION.

YOU KNOW ABOUT THE FARM?

SURE, WHO DOESN'T?

IS IT EVERYTHING THEY SAY?

IS IT TRUE THAT THEY HAVE... **FREE STUFFING** THERE?

AND KINEMATOGRAPH SHOWS ON TUESDAYS?

AND CLAMBAKES?

LOOK, WHAT'S THIS ALL ABOUT? THE FARM'S NO GOOD. IT'S A *PRISON*.

EVERY NON-HUMAN FABLE I KNOW DREAMS OF *NOTHING* BUT LEAVING THE FARM BEHIND.

THAT'S BECAUSE THEY'VE NEVER BEEN IN THE WILD.

IF THEY *HAD*, THEY'D NEVER WANT TO LEAVE THE FARM AGAIN.

IF IT'S SO GREAT, WHY DID YOU MONKEYS LEAVE?

MONKEYS? JESUS CHRIST!

WE WERE NEVER THERE TO BEGIN WITH.

HUH?

"BEFORE THE ADVERSARY CAME, WE LIVED IN PEACE AND COMFORT IN THE HOMELANDS.

"SOME OF US LIVED IN CITIES AND IN TOWNS, WITH ALL THE MODERN CONVENIENCES. WE HAD ARTS, CULTURE, AND REFINEMENT.

"OTHERS AMONG US ONCE DWELT IN PASTORAL SPLENDOR, FREE FROM THE CARES OF URBAN LIFE, IN PEACEFUL TRANQUILITY.

"STILL OTHERS LIVED IN BLISSFUL SIMPLICITY, WITH NO CARES FOR THE FUTURE, NOR SCARS FROM THE PAST."

"THEN THE ADVERSARY CAME, AND WE WERE DRIVEN FROM OUR HOMES.

"FINDING ONE ANOTHER, AND SOMEHOW EVADING CAPTURE, OR WORSE, WE AT LAST REACHED AN UNGUARDED GATEWAY TO THE MUNDANE WORLD.

"WE FOUND OURSELVES IN A JUNGLE, BUT NOT LIKE ANY WE HAD KNOWN. HERE WERE NO PEACEFUL APE CITIES, NO BUCOLIC APE VILLAGES, NO CAREFREE, HARMLESS DAYS.

"WE HAD HEARD STORIES OF THE FARM BEFORE LEAVING OUR HOMELANDS, AND HAD PITIED THE CREATURES INCARCERATED THERE.

"NOW, WE CAN THINK OF NOTHING MORE DESIRABLE THAN A LIFETIME OF SAFETY AND SECLUSION IN SUCH A REFUGE."

BEFORE THE HAIRY LITTLE BASTARDS COULD MAKE THEIR PITCH, THE NEGOTIATIONS WERE INTERRUPTED.

A-AESOP! AESOP!

WHAT IS IT, GEORGE?

HUN... HUNT... HUNT...!

EXCITABLE LITTLE FELLA, ISN'T HE?

NOT NORMALLY--

--HE'S USUALLY JUST CURIOUS.

DEEP BREATHS NOW, GEORGE. WHAT'S THE TROUBLE?

NOBODY MAKE *ANY* SUDDEN MOVES. I'M SURE WE CAN SETTLE THIS PEACEFULLY.

FELLOW HUMANS! I'M NOT WITH THESE *STRANGE* TALK-ING CREATURES, BELIEVE ME. I'M JACK HORNER, HONEST TRAVELER, ONLY JUST PASSING THROUGH.

JACK... HORNER?

THAT'S RIGHT. NOW IF YOU WANT TO ROUND UP THESE *MONKEYS* FOR THEIR LUXURIOUS SKINS, THEIR DELICIOUS BRAINS, *AND* THEIR LUCKY PAWS, I'LL JUST BE ON MY WAY...

SO MUCH FOR THE GENTLE ART OF NEGOTIATION.

22

TURNS OUT THE NEWS OF THE BOUNTY ON MY HEAD IN MOROCCO HAD TRAVELED FARTHER AND FASTER THAN I'D THOUGHT.

THESE GUYS DECIDED IT WAS MORE PROFITABLE TO TRADE ME TO THE AUTHORITIES UP NORTH THAN DEAL WITH A BUNCH OF SMELLY MONKEYS, TALKING OR NO.

NOT THAT I COULD BLAME THEM, BUT STILL...

THEY DIDN'T LEAVE ME ALL ON MY LONESOME, THOUGH. I HAD A CELLMATE. I THOUGHT SHE WAS JUST A CHIMP OF THE MUNDANE, NON-TALKING VARIETY, BUT THEN...

SO WHAT'S *YOUR* NAME, BRIGHT EYES?

HER LEASH WOULDN'T REACH--

--WHICH WAS THE ONLY THING THAT SAVED ME FROM A BIG DOSE OF APE LOVIN'.

PSST! JANE? ARE YOU IN HERE?

AESOP?

IS THAT YOU, HONEY?

WHAT HAVE I *TOLD* YOU ABOUT SINGING IN THE JUNGLE?

I KNOW, BUT WHAT CAN I DO? WHEN THE MOOD STRIKES, IT *STRIKES*.

I FINALLY HAD SOMETHING TO WEAR, AT LEAST. IT WASN'T A PINSTRIPE SUIT, BUT IT BEAT THE BIRTHDAY VARIETY.

WE'RE READY TO LEAVE FOR THE *FARM.*

WHICH WAY DO WE GO?

NOT JUST YET.

WHAT DO YOU MEAN?

I'M NOT READY TO HEAD BACK TO CIVILIZATION *JUST YET.* PARTICULARLY NOT WITH A PRICE ON MY HEAD.

I THINK I'LL JUST STICK AROUND IN THE JUNGLE FOR A WHILE UNTIL THE HEAT DIES DOWN.

AND SINCE *YOU* CAN'T FIND THE FARM WITHOUT ME, THERE ISN'T MUCH YOU CAN DO ABOUT IT, IS THERE?

IF YOU'RE STICKING AROUND, MAYBE *WE* CAN GET BETTER ACQUAINTED, HONEY.

SORRY, JANE.

I'M *STILL* NOT THAT HARD UP.

BUT CHECK BACK WITH ME IN A FEW DAYS AND WE'LL SEE.

A FEW YEARS LATER, I MADE THE MISTAKE OF TELLING A FEW OF MY JUNGLE TALES TO A PENCIL-SHARPENER SALESMAN FROM CHICAGO.

PLEASED TO MEET YOU, EDGAR. I'M JACK.

THE BASTARD WENT ON TO MAKE A MINT PASSING MY STORIES OFF AS HIS OWN.

STILL, IT TAUGHT ME THAT THERE WAS INDEED A FORTUNE TO BE MADE IN HOLLYWOOD.

I DON'T KNOW, JACK--THOSE MOVIES SOUND KINDA *SCARY*. ALL THAT RUNNING AND YELLING? I DON'T KNOW THAT I'D LIKE THEM.

MAYBE AFRICA *ISN'T* SUCH A GOOD IDEA, AFTER ALL.

HOW ABOUT WE HIT A STRIP CLUB INSTEAD?

EEP.

NEXT: WE RESUME OUR REGULARLY SCHEDULED PROGRAMMING ALREADY IN PROGRESS, AS GARY AND I HAVE AN EROTIC ADVENTURE WITH QUEEN BEATRIX OF THE NETHERLANDS, FEND OFF HORDES OF MUTANT VAMPIRE SPACE PIRATES, AND DISCOVER THE TRUE SOURCE OF THE NILE, BECAUSE THAT FECKLESS BASTARD JOHN HANNING SPEKE DIDN'T KNOW HIS *ASS* FROM A HOLE IN THE GROUND.

"THE BASIC HEROIC IDEAL DIDN'T GET RUINED
JUST BECAUSE A **JACKASS** MADE USE OF IT."

JUST *YOU* AND *ME*, GARY, ON OUR OWN AGAIN, AS IT SHOULD BE.

NO MORE FABLETOWN, OR THE *FARM*. NO MORE EX-GIRLFRIENDS TRYING TO SLEEP THEMSELVES INTO A HAPPY LITTLE DEPRESSION COMA.

NO MORE ANGRY GODS OF LITERATURE TRYING TO DESTROY THE WORLD.

NOTHING BUT THE WIDE ROAD AHEAD OF US, *PREGNANT* WITH THE PROMISE OF ADVENTURE.

WHY, THAT WAS *QUITE* THE POETIC TURN OF PHRASE, GENERAL JACK. I'M SINCERELY TOUCHED.

AND I'M SINCERELY TIRED.

EXHAUSTED, IN FACT. HOW MANY DAYS HAVE WE BEEN HOOFING IT ALONG THESE COUNTRY ROADS?

ABOUT TWO HOURS IS ALL. COULD IT *BE* YOU'RE MORE TIRED THAN USUAL BECAUSE YOU'VE LET YOURSELF GO TO FAT?

FAT JACK

THE NEW ADVENTURES OF JACK AND JACK

Part 1 of 4

WELL, THIS IS JUST A *THEORY* BUT, REMEMBER HOW, WHEN YOU QUIT A FEW ISSUES BACK, YOU SAID YOU WERE TAKING YOUR FAVORITE *ARTIST* WITH YOU?

ONLY NOW IT'S THAT *OTHER* ARTIST'S TURN AGAIN. WHAT IF HE'S MAD THAT YOU CHOSE FAVORITES AND IS GETTING *RE-VENGE* BY DRAWING YOU UGLY?

HUH?

FAVORITE ARTIST? SOMEONE DRAWING ME? WHAT SORT OF INSANE *NONSENSE* ARE YOU TALKING ABOUT, GARY?

UH....

I HAVE NO *IDEA* WHAT I JUST SAID.

THAT'S WEIRD, HUH?

WHAT *WERE* WE TALKING ABOUT?

I'M NOT SURE. YOU SAID I WAS *FAT* AND THEN YOU SAID SOMETHING ABOUT WHY YOU *THOUGHT* I WAS FAT, BUT I THINK IT WAS ALL WEIRD GOOFY CRAP.

ONLY NOW I CAN'T RECALL WHAT IT WAS.

THAT'S ODD. I CAN'T REMEMBER *EITHER.*

SO, *WHY* DO YOU THINK YOU'RE GETTING FAT, JACK?

WHO KNOWS? BUT IT'S TIRING ME OUT.

WHY ARE WE WALKING, LIKE PENNILESS **SUCKERS** ANYWAY, WHEN WE COULD BE RIDING ALONG IN STYLE?

WHY DON'T YOU **SWEET TALK** THE ROCKS AND TREES AND WHIP US UP A FLINTSTONE CAR TO TAKE THE LOAD OFF OUR TIRED DOGS?

TALK TO ROCKS? TALK TO TREES? ARE YOU **SERIOUS**, GENERAL JACK?

I CAN'T DO THAT.

I MEAN SURE, I COULD DO IT. ANYONE CAN TALK TO ANYTHING THEY LIKE.

BUT ROCKS AND TREES COULDN'T ANSWER BACK, BECAUSE--WELL, THEY'RE ROCKS AND TREES.

WHAT WERE YOU THINKING?

TO TELL YOU THE TRUTH, GARY, I'VE NO IDEA. IT'S LIKE I'M TRYING TO REMEMBER THINGS I JUST KNEW A MOMENT AGO, BUT THEY'RE SUDDENLY GONE.

FRUSTRATING, HUH?

EARLY MORNING IN THE CATSKILLS...

PACK UP, PRIS, HILL. WE *REALLY* SHOULD BE MOVING ALONG, BEFORE THE MUNDYS START RETURNING.

REMEMBER TO PACK UP ALL THE GUNS, TOO. BURY THE ONES WE CAN'T CARRY.

YOU TOO, JACK. WAKE UP. *GET UP.* GET PACKED. WE NEED TO GET OUT OF HERE.

PACK WHAT? I OWN *NOTHING.* EVEN THE CLOTHES ON MY BACK ARE A FABRICATION OF MY BORROWED POWER.

OH, YOU'RE UP.

HEY, WHAT'S WRONG WITH YOU *NOW?* WHY SO GLUM, CHUM?

I KNOW WE NEED TO LEAVE, ROBIN, BUT WHERE TO? WHERE DO I *BELONG* IN THIS VAST UNIVERSE?

WELL, THAT'S SORT OF A BIG *QUESTION,* ISN'T IT? I TAKE IT YOU DON'T WANT TO GO HOME?

NO. THE CASTLE IN WHICH I WAS RAISED AND KEPT ALMOST A PRISONER FOR SO MANY CENTURIES IS NO LONGER OF ANY INTEREST TO ME.

NOT GOING BACK TO THE FARM AND SEE YOUR FATHER AGAIN, NOW THAT YOU DID THE HEROIC *DEED* HE REQUIRED, BEFORE BEING ALLOWED TO CONFRONT HIM?

NO. WHAT A NAÏVE FOOL I WAS TO BELIEVE THAT *LOAD* OF DUNG.

HARD FOR ME TO FAULT HIM FOR THAT ONE, SINCE IT *DID* RESULT IN SAVING ALL OF US. BUT YEAH, JACK HORNER IS *QUITE* THE BULLSHIT ARTIST.

MY FATHER IS A **COMPLETE** SCOUNDREL AND TAWDRY HUCKSTER AT BEST, AND A TRULY WICKED MAN, BY MOST MEASURES.

MY MOTHER IS, BY ALL ACCOUNTS, **ENTIRELY** EVIL.

WE KEPT PRETTY CLOSE TRACK OF HER, KID. I HATE TO SAY THIS, BUT THE SNOW QUEEN IS INDEED A BAD ONE.

AND ALMOST AS MUCH A STRANGER TO ME AS MY FATHER. SHE'S BEEN ABSENT FOR **MOST** OF MY LIFE, LIVING FAR AWAY AT THE SEAT OF THE EMPIRE.

I SHOULD FEEL EXULTANT NOW, HAVING JUST TAKEN PART IN THE SAVING OF **EVERYTHING** THAT EXISTS.

BUT INSTEAD I'M OVERCOME WITH THE MELANCHOLY OF THE **NEWLY** ORPHANED.

HEY, JACK, DON'T GET SHAKESPEAREAN ON US. YOU'RE NOT **THAT** BAD OFF.

TRUTH IS, I WAS ALWAYS AN ORPHAN. A SIMPERING **TOADY** NAMED VRUMPUS WAS MY ONLY FATHER AND OUR CASTLE'S **LIBRARY** MY ONLY MOTHER.

QUIT FEELING SORRY FOR YOURSELF, JACK. SNAP OUT OF IT! LIFE ISN'T PERFECT? SO WHAT? TRILLIONS OF PEOPLE HAVE IT **WORSE** THAN YOU DO.

WANT TO KNOW YOUR PLACE IN THE UNIVERSE? FINE. I'LL TELL YOU WHAT IT IS. I'LL GIVE YOU THE **ONLY** WORD OF ADVICE THAT'S ANY DAMN GOOD.

FIGURE OUT WHAT YOU WANT TO DO AND *DO IT.* THAT'S IT. THAT'S ALL I HAVE TO OFFER.

YOU CAME HERE ALL EXCITED ABOUT BEING A HERO, SO GO *BE* ONE. WHO CARES IF YOUR LOUSY FATHER TRICKED YOU INTO IT?

THE WORD, THE CONCEPT, THE BASIC HEROIC IDEAL DIDN'T GET RUINED JUST BECAUSE A *JACKASS* MADE USE OF IT.

SO, GO OUT AND WANDER THE MANY WORLDS. SLAY DRAGONS. OVERTHROW EVIL WARLORDS. RESCUE HOT MAIDENS FROM DARK TOWERS.

OR *DON'T.* BE WHO AND WHATEVER YOU WANT TO BE. GO FAIL AT A FEW THINGS AND THEN TRY OTHER THINGS INSTEAD. YOU'VE GOT *PLENTY* OF TIME.

BUT *QUIT* WHINING ABOUT HOW BAD YOUR RELATIONS ARE. I'M PART OF THE SAME EXTENDED FAMILY OF JERKS AND REPROBATES, REMEMBER?

IF YOU GET LONELY FOR FAMILY--FOR THE FEW STILL-DECENT TWIGS OF THE OLD FAMILY TREE-- THEN LOOK UP YOUR AUNTS AGAIN.

THE EVER-FABULOUS *PAGE SISTERS* WILL ALWAYS BE AROUND SOMEWHERE. WE'VE GOT OUR OWN DESTINIES TO WORK OUT, AFTER ALL.

AND SO, QUITE PROPERLY CHASTENED, I SET OUT ON THE ROAD TO ADVENTURE.

FIRST STOP: THE DEAD HEART OF THE EVIL EMPIRE.

39

HUH?

BUT WHAT A CHANGED *MAN* "MYSELF" HAS BECOME.

IT SEEMS THE POWERS LEFT A PERMANENT MARK, EVEN DURING THEIR SHORT DURATION.

HEY, KID?

NOT ALL OF THE WINTER RETURNED TO MY MOTHER. SOME PART OF IT LINGERS, BEYOND MY ABILITY TO DISCHARGE IT. IS SOME SMALL FRAGMENT OF IT MINE BY NATURE?

I DON'T KNOW IF YOU REALIZE IT, BUT THIS *ISN'T* A SAFE PLACE ANYMORE.

HELLO?

I'M STILL STRONGER THAN I USED TO BE. TOUGHER. AND I CAN TELL THE ABILITY TO MOVE BETWEEN WORLDS IS STILL INSIDE OF ME.

ARE THESE NATURAL ABILITIES THAT I WOULD HAVE DEVELOPED IN TIME, AND ONLY TRIGGERED BY RECENT EVENTS?

HEY, FLESH BOY, YOU REALLY *SHOULD* GET YOUR HEAD OUT OF YOUR SHIT-SPITTER AND START PAYING *ATTENTION* TO THE DANGEROUS WORLD AROUND YOU.

I PLAYED SCENES JUST LIKE THIS IN MY MIND A THOUSAND TIMES OR MORE.

YOW!

HE GOT ME!

HYAUUGGH!

I IMAGINED MYSELF A BOLD AND RECKLESS HERO, JUST LIKE THOSE CONFIDENT, SWAGGERING, DEVIL-MAY-CARE CHARACTERS IN MY STORYBOOKS.

I NEVER IMAGINED THE BRUTALITY, THE MAD PHYSICAL EXERTION, AND THE NEARLY PARALYZING FEAR.

WATCH OUT! WATCH OUT!

YOU'RE BREAKING ME!

I COULD ACTUALLY DIE, RIGHT HERE, RIGHT NOW.

GRANTED, I ALSO COULD HAVE DIED, ALONG WITH EVERYONE ELSE, IN THAT RECENT BUSINESS WITH KEVIN THORN.

BUT THAT WAS SOMETHING LESS IMMEDIATE. IT WAS AN IMPERSONAL FATE THAT COULD HAVE SCOOPED ME UP WITHOUT MY KNOWLEDGE OR DIRECT INVOLVEMENT.

THIS IS A REAL FIGHT, WITH BLOOD AND PAIN AND VERY IMMEDIATE, TACTILE, ANIMAL DANGER. VICIOUS AND BARBARIC.

MY BLOOD AND MY PAIN!

A MINUTE EARLIER, WHEN I STILL POSSESSED THE POWERS OF A GOD, I COULD HAVE DESTROYED THEM ALL WITH A WAVE OF MY HAND.

BAD TIMING, HUH?

STILL, I GOT A STORYBOOK ENDING.

"AND HOW CAN MAN DIE BETTER, THAN FACING FEARFUL ODDS, FOR THE ASHES OF HIS FATHERS, AND THE TEMPLES OF HIS GODS?"

UUUUGHHH.

ARE YOU DEAD, BOY?

UH....

I GUESS NOT.

THE DEAD CAN'T *POSSIBLY* FEEL THIS MUCH PAIN.

TRUTH BE TOLD, I DON'T KNOW HOW YOU *MEAT* PEOPLE CAN GET THROUGH A SINGLE DAY.

EVERY STRAY SCRATCH BLEEDS AND CAUSES YOU AGONY AND CAN EVEN KILL YOU STONE DEAD, WITHOUT IMMEDIATE TREATMENT.

IF I GET WHACKED WITH A SWORD--WHICH I WAS, ONCE OR TWICE JUST NOW--THE MOST I NEED IS A BIT OF GLUE AND SANDING TO BE FINE AGAIN.

HNNGGGH.

I'M *SO* HAPPY FOR YOU.

SARCASM, RIGHT? MY *MAKER* EMPLOYED SARCASM ONCE IN A WHILE.

SORRY. I SHOULDN'T BE RUDE TO SOMEONE WHO JUST RISKED HIMSELF TO HELP ME. I APOLOGIZE.

I'M JACK FROST. WHOM DO I HAVE THE PLEASURE OF ADDRESSING?

I'M NOT SURE. IF I HAVE A NAME, IT'S SIMPLY OWL. THAT'S ALL MY MAKER EVER CALLED ME ON THOSE RARE OCCASIONS WHEN HE ADDRESSED ME DIRECTLY.

HE'S GONE NOW. BEEN GONE FOR MONTHS. I IMAGINE HE TOOK WHAT PASSED FOR MY NAME WITH HIM.

I'M BEGINNING TO SUSPECT HE ISN'T COMING BACK. I'VE BEEN WAITING IN THE GENERAL AREA, IN CASE HE DOES.

AND HELPING THE ODD YOUNG PASSERBY WITH ARMED VILLAINS?

MOST HAVE THE SENSE TO AVOID THESE BANDS OF VILLAINS, DESERTERS AND SCAVENGERS. BUT NO, I DON'T USUALLY INTERFERE.

MY MAKER NEVER LIKED GOBS AND SUCH, AND WOULDN'T ABIDE MILITARY DESERTERS, SO IN DEFERENCE TO HIM, I SUPPOSE, I PICKED A SIDE AND JUMPED IN.

I'M NOT NORMALLY SO IMPETUOUS.

WELL, YOU HAVE MY UNDYING GRATITUDE, SIR. IF I CAN EVER BE OF SERVICE TO YOU...

YOU CAN. JUST UP THOSE HILLS IS A REMOTE WOODSHOP. *DESERTED* NOW. THERE ARE TOOLS YOU CAN USE TO REPAIR ME. WOOD RASPS AND SANDING STONES AND SUCH.

IF YOU AREN'T SKILLED IN WOODWORKING, I CAN DIRECT YOU. I JUST DON'T HAVE THE ARMS, FINGERS AND OPPOSABLE *THUMB* TO DO IT FOR MYSELF.

A VERY REASONABLE REQUEST, FOR SO BRAVE AND NOBLE A RAPTOR. I'LL BE *HAPPY* TO HELP.

LEAD ON, *MacDUFF.*

MacDUFF? WHO'S THAT?

UHM....

YOU.

IF YOU WANT TO BE.

FEW HOURS LATER...

THERE. *YEAH.* JUST LIKE THAT. PERFECT!

THANK YOU, JACK FROST. A TOUCH OF *PAINT* AND I'LL BE GOOD AS NEW AGAIN.

I'M HAPPY I COULD BE OF HELP.

AND LOOK AT *YOU.* ALL OF YOUR WOUNDS ARE REPAIRED ALREADY. YOU'RE NOT LIKE MOST MEAT PEOPLE. THEY EXPIRE ALL THE TIME FROM WOUNDS SUCH AS YOU HAD.

ONE OF THE ADVANTAGES HANDED DOWN FROM MY *UNLIKELY* PARENTAGE.

HOLD STILL FOR JUST A DAB OR TWO...

NOW THAT YOUR DEBT TO ME IS PAID, WHERE WILL YOU GO NEXT?

SOMEWHERE I'M *NEEDED,* TO HELP GOOD PEOPLE FROM BAD ONES, LIKE THOSE WHO ATTACKED ME DOWN AT THE CITY.

SOMEWHERE A CAPTIVE NEEDS RESCUING, OR A MONSTER NEEDS KILLING, AND WRONGS NEED *RIGHTING.*

I'VE DECIDED TO ENTER THE *HERO* TRADE.

"My partner and I are **very** serious about the hero profession."

Following the incident at the great city of thorns, Jack and his new companion set off on foot for the rural districts northeast of the imperial capital. Most Jack scholars set this period as the beginning of his career, universally discounting his occasional mentions of an incident in the American Adirondacks as a fabrication.
– From: "A Probable Outline of Jack Frost's Life and Adventures" by Wulf Alondair Lathe

Baby Steps Along the Glory Road
THE NEW ADVENTURES OF JACK AND JACK Part 2 of 4

NEW PETTY CONQUERORS SPRINGING UP EVERYWHERE, TO TAKE ADVANTAGE OF THE SUDDEN DISSOLUTION OF CENTRAL AUTHORITY.

HERE, GERTRUDE!

SEE? IT WAS A CHALLENGE TO FIGHT, NOT AN INVITATION TO LEAD THE WAY.

COUNTLESS VILLAINS AND MONSTERS LET LOOSE ON LANDS AND VILLAGES LONG UNUSED TO DEFENDING THEMSELVES.

SO WHAT'S YOUR POINT?

DO YOU NOT *LIKE* YOUR NAME? THEN PICK ANOTHER ONE.

MacDUFF AND I SHOULD HAVE BEEN ALMOST LITERALLY TRIPPING OVER THE GOOD CAUSES WORTH TAKING ON, THE BATTLES WORTH FIGHTING.

NO, I LIKE MY NAME FINE. BUT IT DOESN'T ACTUALLY *DERIVE* FROM WHAT YOU SAID.

WHICH RAISES THE QUESTION: IS MY NAME *TRULY* LEGITIMATE?

AH HA. A CLUE!

BUT HERE'S A TIMELESS TRUTH WE HAD TO DISCOVER FOR OURSELVES-- THE HARD WAY.

"LEAD ON, MacDUFF," IS A COMMON AND PERFECTLY *ACCEPTABLE* PHRASE. IT APPEARS IN IMPORTANT WORKS OF FACT AND FICTION FROM A DOZEN DIFFERENT WORLDS.

IN ANY AGRARIAN SOCIETY--OR ANY SORT OF SOCIETY AT ALL FOR THAT MATTER--THE INSTANCES OF VILLAINS, OR MONSTERS, OR LAWLESS ROBBER WARLORDS NEEDING TO BE SLAIN ARE RELATIVELY FEW AND FAR BETWEEN.

EVEN IF IT WAS *ORIGINALLY* A MISQUOTATION, IT'S EARNED ITS OWN PLACE IN ANY IDIOMATIC PANTHEON.

EVEN IN THE WORST OF TIMES, MOST FOLKS SIMPLY DIDN'T ENCOUNTER SUCH TROUBLES ON A FREQUENT BASIS.

TRUST ME, FRIEND. YOUR NAME AND ITS ORIGIN ARE *ENTIRELY* SOUND.

HERE, GERTRUDE!

INSTEAD THEIR MOST COMMON TRIBULATIONS INCLUDED A MISSING MILK GOAT.

OR FROST-DAMAGED CROPS THAT NEEDED TO BE HARVESTED IMMEDIATELY, TO KEEP THEM FROM ROTTING IN THE FIELD.

OR GETTING ONE OF THEIR PIGS UNSTUCK FROM A DITCH.

NOT THE *MOST* HEROIC OF WEEKS, HUH, JACK?

YOU COULD BE MORE HELPFUL, YOU KNOW.

HOW? I'M HARDLY BUILT TO CHOP FIREWOOD, OR PULL PIGS, OR DO AUGHT OTHER OF THE FREE CHORES FOR FAT LANDOWNERS YOU *CONSTANTLY* LET YOUR-SELF GET TALKED INTO DOING.

WELL, WE DO USUALLY GET A HEARTY MEAL OUT OF IT, AND SOME-TIMES A COMFY HAYLOFT TO SLEEP IN.

AND *HOW* EXACTLY DOES THAT BENEFIT ME?

I NEITHER EAT NOR SLEEP.

TRUE, BUT SINCE YOU CONTRIBUTED ABSOLUTELY *NOTHING* TOWARDS EARNING THE FOOD AND SHELTER, IT BALANCES OUT NICELY, DOESN'T IT?

MacDUFF WAS RIGHT, OF COURSE. HE'S OLD AND WISE, AND SURPRISINGLY WELL READ.

AH, *THERE* YOU ARE, GERTRUDE.

THE FARMERS AND SIMPLE TOWNSFOLK WERE TAKING ADVANTAGE OF MY EAGERNESS TO PERFORM GOOD DEEDS.

COME ALONG HOME NOW. MOTHER BENECOSTA NEEDS THE MILK.

I NEEDED TO WORK OUT SOME WAY TO FIND OUT WHERE THE REAL TROUBLES WERE OCCURRING--WHERE PEOPLE IN ACTUAL MORTAL JEOPARDY NEED A HERO.

HELP ME PUSH THIS DAMNED *GOAT*, MacDUFF!

HOW?

NO HANDS, NO ARMS, REMEMBER?

WHY NOT USE THE SAME METHODS THOSE IN OTHER, LESS ADVENTUROUS OCCUPATIONS EMPLOY TO DRUM UP BUSINESS?

PECK HER IN HER *BUTT!* THAT'LL GET HER GOING!

I MOST *CERTAINLY* WILL NOT!

I'M A SCHOLAR AND A COMPANION TO EMPERORS!

WHY NOT ADVERTISE?

I WILL NOT RISK GETTING DUNG ON MY *HANDSOME* BEAK.

AW, FORGET IT. THIS IS USELESS!

AS SOON AS I BUILD UP ENOUGH MAGIC POWER TO MAKE ANOTHER JUMP BETWEEN WORLDS, WE'RE GOING TO A PLACE WITH *PRINTING* TECHNOLOGY!

POSTERS? YEAH, WE CAN PRINT YOU UP A BUNCH OF POSTERS.

BLACK AND WHITE. FOUR COLOR. OR ANYTHING IN BETWEEN.

CUTE TOY OWL, BY THE WAY. MUST BE *HELL* ON BATTERIES.

AND A SIDE ORDER OF MEATLOAF, TOO.

HARDWARE

BAKER & SONS PRINTING

FLYERS, HANDBILLS, INVITATIONS, JOB PRINTING

A SIDE ORDER OF MEATLOAF TO GO WITH THE MEATLOAF DINNER?

YEAH, IT SAYS RIGHT HERE THAT THE MEAL COMES WITH *TWO* SIDE ORDERS, SO I WANT ONE SIDE ORDER OF MASHED POTATOES--EXTRA GRAVY--AND ONE SIDE ORDER OF MEATLOAF.

UHM... I'LL HAVE THE--

True home cooking that doesn't mess up your own kitchen

NO SHIRT, NO SHOES, NO SIR!

SEXY

Panel 1 (boy ordering): I'M NOT SURE-- AND CHOCOLATE CREAM PIE. NOT JUST A SLICE-- A *WHOLE* PIE. AND I THINK I'LL HAVE THE FRIED CHICKEN DINNER, TOO.

AND MY TWO SIDE ORDERS FOR THAT WILL BE MASHED POTATOES AND *MORE* FRIED CHICKEN.

JUST A MOMENT, SIR. I THINK I'LL HAVE TO CHECK WITH THE MANAGER.

HOLD ON THERE, MISSY. WE'RE NOT DONE *YET.* MY LITTLE BUDDY HASN'T ORDERED.

I THINK I'LL HAVE THE--

ADD YOUR ORDER TO MINE, GARY, AND THEN PAY FOR EVERYTHING. I'LL BE IN THE JOHN TRYING TO *DUMP* SOME OF THIS LOAD.

MY TURN TO PAY *AGAIN,* JACK?

YOU GOTTA DO YOUR PART, PALOMINO. IT'S THE SIDEKICK'S *DUTY* TO--

BUT I'M ALREADY THE ONE WHO HAS TO GET THE DAY JOBS, AND PAY FOR EVERYTHING, AND PAY FOR THE MOTEL ROOMS...

...WHILE YOU LAZE AROUND THE *POOL* ALL THE DING DANG TIME!

I CAN'T DO *MANUAL* LABOR. LOOK AT ME!

I'M BIG AS A *HOUSE!* PUT ME TO WORK AND IT'S HEART ATTACK CITY!

YOU COULD EAT *LESS.*

YOU'D THINK SO, BUT YOU'D BE WRONG. TRUTH IS, I CAN'T SEEM TO EAT *ENOUGH.* NO MATTER HOW MUCH I GOBBLE DOWN, I'M STILL *ALWAYS* HUNGRY.

SEXY

I THINK THERE'S A THING GOING ON!

A THING?

YEAH, YOU KNOW, A *THING!* I NEVER USED TO HAVE AN EATING PROBLEM BEFORE, AND NEVER GAINED AN INCH, NO MATTER HOW MUCH I *DID* EAT.

BUT NOW EVERYTHING I EAT GETS PACKED ON IN EXTRA TONNAGE. I THINK SOMEONE'S DOING *SOMETHING* TO ME.

WELL, PEOPLE'S METABOLISMS CHANGE AS THEY GET OLDER, JACK.

NOT ME!

FABLES DON'T GET OLDER.

AND I'M STILL THE MOST POPULAR, POWERFUL FABLE IN THE ENTIRE WORLD, SO I SHOULD BE *DOUBLY* IMMUNE.

BUT ALL OF THIS IS JUST WATER UNDER THE BRIDGE-- WHICH REMINDS ME, I HAVE TO PISS SOMETHING *FIERCE,* TOO.

SO PAY THE CHECK AND I'LL MEET YOU AT THE TABLE, ONCE I DROP THE KIDS OFF AT THE POOL.

BUT--

THAT'S **NOT** AN EXPLANA-TION!

WELL, IT'S LIKE **THIS**. EVERY TIME I GET RICH, SOMEONE OR SOMETHING HAPPENS TO TAKE IT ALL AWAY FROM ME.

OR I SPEND IT ALL ON FAST CARS AND FAST WOMEN AND SUCH.

SOMEHOW OR OTHER I **ALWAYS** LOSE IT.

BUT THAT'S NOT GOING TO HAPPEN THIS TIME. THIS TIME I WILL NEVER LOSE **ANY** OF MY FABULOUS WEALTH, AS LONG AS I NEVER EVER SPEND A DIME OF IT.

THEN I'LL ALWAYS HAVE THE SAME BIG FORTUNE, AS LONG AS NO ONE LEARNS I'VE GOT IT, SO **PLEASE** KEEP **QUIET** ABOUT THE **GOLD!**

BUT HOW ARE WE GOING TO PAY FOR THIS MEAL, JACK?

JOE'S DINER MAMA JOE'S

"YOU'LL THINK OF SOMETHING. I'VE GOT CONFIDENCE IN YOU, BUDDY."

TRY THE FRIED CHICKEN AT MAMA JOE'S

ELSEWHERE...

"IF YOU ARE TRULY THE HERO YOU CLAIM, THEN HEED MY TALE.

"IN THE PAST, THE FOREST KILLERS SERVED THE IMPERIAL SOLDIERS, ARMIES OF MONSTERS TO ENFORCE THE EMPIRE'S WILL IN THIS WORLD.

"AS SUCH THEY WERE CONTROLLED, ONLY LET LOOSE IN THE NIGHT TO PUNISH SOME OFFENDER AGAINST LAW AND ORDER.

"BUT NOW THAT THE IMPERIAL SOLDIERS ARE GONE, THE NIGHT WALKERS PREY UPON WHOMEVER THEY WISH."

"AND IN THE DEEP GLOOM OF THE FOREST, THEY CAN SOMETIMES COME OUT IN THE DAY.

"IN THE PAST THE EMPIRE ALWAYS MAINTAINED SAFE PATHS AND ROADWAYS IN THE WOODS, SPELL-GUARDED AGAINST THE NIGHT WALKERS."

YERP!

OW! OOF! OW!

"BUT THOSE SPELLS HAVEN'T BEEN MAINTAINED. THEY'VE BEGUN BREAKING DOWN.

"THE MONSTERS ATTACKED MY FATHER'S HOLDFAST, *MERVEILLEUX GARDE.*

"I RODE OUT TWO DAYS AGO TO FIND RESCUE, GOLDEN SLIPPER BEING THE FASTEST RIDING CROOT IN OUR STABLES.

JACK

MONSTERS FOUGHT

contact at

"BUT THE FOREST MONSTERS OVER-TOOK US."

SO, ARE *YOU* THE HERO OF THIS NOTICE, MR. FROST?

CAN YOU HELP US?

OF COURSE. MacDUFF AND I WILL DO *WHATEVER* WE CAN, MISS FEN.

THAT IS, AFTER ALL, THE *BUSINESS* WE'RE IN.

ESPECIALLY IF YOUR DILEMMA INCLUDES A MISSING MILK GOAT, OR A PIG STUCK IN A DITCH.

WHAT? I DON'T UNDERSTAND.

WHAT IS A "PIG," OR A "GOAT?" THESE WORDS MEAN NOTHING TO ME.

PLEASE *EXCUSE* MY PARTNER, MISS.

HE WAS ATTEMPTING TO EASE YOUR MIND AND LIGHTEN THE *MOOD* WITH HUMOR. BUT HIS JOKE DOESN'T REALLY *TRANSLATE* IN THIS WORLD.

YOU'RE *HARDLY* BEING HELPFUL, MacDUFF.

NO, I SUPPOSE *NOT.* FORGIVE ME, JACK. IT WON'T HAPPEN AGAIN.

TRUTH IS, MY PARTNER AND I ARE *VERY* SERIOUS ABOUT THE HERO PROFESSION, MISS.

AH YES, YOUR PROFESSION.

WHAT WILL YOUR FEE *BE* FOR RESCUING US, MR. FROST?

NO CHARGE WHATSOEVER, MISS.

WE AREN'T IN THIS BUSINESS TO MAKE *MONEY.*

WE'RE **HEROES,** NOT MERCENARIES.

WE HAVE DIFFERENT SOURCES OF INCOME TO SUSTAIN US BETWEEN HEROIC QUESTS.

I DON'T KNOW **WHAT** YOU'RE BLATHERING ON ABOUT, JACK FROST.

BUT I FEAR YOUR INCOME IS ABOUT TO BE IN DIRE JEOPARDY IF YOU DON'T GET **BACK** INTO THE KITCHEN AND HEROICALLY WASH THOSE DIRTY DISHES.

IF MR. KRUMPER FINDS YOU SITTING OUT **HERE** AMONG THE CUSTOMERS...

AH YES, BEATRICE. THANK YOU FOR REMINDING ME.

PLEASE GO TELL MR. KRUMPLER TO ASSEMBLE MY WAGES TO DATE. I WILL NO **LONGER** BE WASHING DISHES HERE.

THE QUEST HAS **BEGUN!**

SHALL WE BE OFF, MISS FEN?

THE DAY GROWS OLDER EVERY **MINUTE** WE DELAY.

NOT TO BE MERCENARY, JACK, BUT HOW MUCH DID WE END UP WITH-- *WAGES* WISE?

NOTHING.

NOTHING?

AFTER MR. KRUMPLER DEDUCTED THE COST OF FOOD AND BOARD, THERE WASN'T MUCH LEFT.

IN LIEU OF COIN I TOOK OUR REMAINING PAY IN TRADE FOR THE SUPPLIES REQUIRED FOR OUR *CURRENT* JOURNEY.

SO WE'RE BROKE *AGAIN?*

NOT AT ALL. WE'VE FOOD TO SUSTAIN US-- WELL, ELSA AND I--FLINT AND TINDER, A TIN FRYING PAN, WARM BLANKETS, *AND* A NEW TENT TO KEEP THE RAIN OFF.

LIFE IS *GOOD*, ALL THINGS CONSIDERED.

GOOD?

NOT TO MAKE *LIGHT* OF YOUR FAMILY'S PERIL, MISS FEN.

PARDON ME, BUT YOU SEEM WORRIED, MISS FEN.

WE ENTERED THE FOREST *LATE* IN THE DAY. THE NIGHT WALKERS WILL BE OUT SOON.

WE COULDN'T AFFORD NOT TO PROCEED. WE NEED TO MAKE *HASTE* TO GET YOU BACK TO YOUR FATHER'S STRONGHOLD.

BUT WE'LL KEEP AN EYE OUT FOR A DEFENSIBLE PLACE IN WHICH TO SPEND THE NIGHT, AND MOVE OUT AGAIN AT *FIRST* LIGHT.

LATER...

YES, THIS IS PROBABLY THE SAFEST PLACE, WITH ONLY ONE EASILY GUARDED ENTRANCE. BUT THE SMELL--AND LOOK AT THE *BONES.*

I THINK THIS IS ONE OF THE MONSTER'S DAY LAIRS.

WHAT WILL BECOME OF US IF THE CREATURE *RETURNS* BEFORE WE LEAVE?

DON'T WORRY YOURSELF, MISS. TRY TO GET SOME SLEEP. MacDUFF NEEDS NONE AND WILL GIVE US *PLENTY* OF WARNING BEFORE ANY DANGER CAN APPROACH.

WE SLEPT ONLY FITFULLY THAT NIGHT, AND STARTED OUT EARLY AGAIN THE NEXT DAY. NONE OF US WANTED TO RISK MEETING THE CAVE'S TRUE OWNER IN PASSING.

WE'RE GETTING *CLOSE.*

AND NONE OF THE MONSTERS HAVE TROUBLED US SO FAR.

TRUE, BUT I *WONDER* IF THAT'S GOOD NEWS. IF THEY AREN'T OUT AND ABOUT, BEING GENERALLY MONSTROUS, WHERE ARE THEY?

WHAT ARE THEY UP TO?

DURING THE DAYS OF THE EMPIRE, THE NIGHT WALKERS WOULD ONLY ASSEMBLE IN GREAT *FORCE* AT THE BEHEST OF THE MILITARY GOVERNORS.

THE IMPERIAL SORCERERS HAD SOME *WAY* TO COMPEL THEM TO DO SO.

OTHERWISE THEY TENDED TO BE SOLITARY, TERRITORIAL, ONLY GATHERING IN *SMALL* PACKS.

BUT THE EMPIRE SOLDIERS AND SORCERERS HAVE BEEN GONE FOR A YEAR OR MORE.

MAYBE IT'S TAKING THE CREATURES TIME TO *ADJUST* BACK TO THEIR OLD WAYS.

POSSIBLY.

BUT I DON'T HAVE A GOOD FEELING ABOUT THIS. HOW INTELLIGENT *ARE* THESE THINGS?

LATE ON THE SECOND DAY WE MADE IT TO *MERVEILLEUX GARDE.*

THERE IT IS! MY *FATHER'S* HOLDFAST!

BUT IT DOESN'T LOOK RIGHT. EVEN FROM *THIS* DISTANCE I CAN TELL SOMETHING'S WRONG.

WE HURRIED THE LAST FEW MILES, ANXIOUS TO GET INSIDE BEFORE NIGHTFALL.

IT'S DESERTED!

WHERE ARE MY FATHER AND MOTHER? WHERE ARE MY SISTERS, AND OUR GUARDS-MEN?

WAS I TOO *LATE?* ARE THEY ALL SLAIN?

IT'S PRETTY CLEAR THERE WAS A RECENT BATTLE OF *SOME* KIND HERE.

BUT NO BODIES OF MAN NOR BEAST, AND DAMNED LITTLE BLOOD.

ODD.

ODD OR NOT, WE'D BEST STAY *HERE* FOR THE NIGHT, WHICH IS FAST APPROACHING.

AND FIND A GOOD PLACE TO MAKE A STAND IF NEED BE.

"THAT'S JUST A FACT OF LIFE.
MONSTERS NEED TO BE CONTROLLED, OR KILLED."

IN A WORLD ON THE FAR EDGES OF THE RECENTLY DESTROYED EMPIRE, I'D TAKEN A JOB WORKING FOR A YOUNG LADY NAMED ELSA FEN.

MORE OF THE PINK SKINS HAVE OCCUPIED THE STONE NEST!

ATTACK!

IT SEEMS HER FAMILY WAS BESET BY A BUNCH OF RAVENING MONSTERS CALLED NIGHT WALKERS--AMONG OTHER LESS COMPLIMENTARY NAMES.

WHERE ARE FATHER AND MOTHER? WHAT HAPPENED TO MY FAMILY AND OUR ARMS-MEN?

A FEW SHORT MOMENTS AGO WE ARRIVED AT HER FAMILY STRONGHOLD TO FIND THE PLACE DESERTED, RIFE WITH RECENT SIGNS OF DESPERATE STRUGGLE.

NOT TO BE CALLOUS, BUT I SUSPECT THE MONSTERS GOT THEM.

OR AM I THE ONLY ONE THAT HEARS ALL THE BESTIAL GROWLING JUST OUTSIDE THE WALLS?

Twice the Hero

❧ THE NEW ADVENTURES OF JACK AND JACK Part 3 of 4 ❧

MEANWHILE-- IN ANOTHER FOREST IN ANOTHER WORLD...

JUST YESTERDAY-- AND THE DAY BEFORE, AND THE DAY BEFORE--YOU WERE COMPLAINING HOW YOU'RE A BIG HEART ATTACK JUST *WAITING* TO HAPPEN.

THAT'S WHY YOU COULDN'T HELP ME DO MY *SWEEPING* AT THE MOTEL TO PAY FOR OUR ROOMS.

YOU COULDN'T EVEN HOLD A DUSTPAN, BECAUSE YOU WERE *AFRAID* EVEN BENDING OVER WOULD BRING ON THE SO-CALLED "BIG ONE."

YEAH? SO? WHAT'S YOUR *POINT?*

NO FAT CHICKS

AND SUDDENLY TODAY YOU ABSOLUTELY NEED TO GO CLIMBING STEEP HILLS IN THE MIDDLE OF NOWHERE? THAT MAKES *NO* SENSE!

ON THE CONTRARY, GARY, OLD PAL, IT MAKES *PERFECT* SENSE. THIS AREA IS FAMOUS FOR ITS MILLION-BAZILLION CAVES. A *REAL* TOURIST ATTRACTION.

SO?

SO, I WANT TO SEE ONE. MAYBE EVEN DISCOVER A NEW ONE AND GET *FAMOUS*.

DON'T LOOK SO DUMBFOUNDED. IF WE WERE IN *ROME* WE'D LOOK AT THE MONUMENTS. IF WE WERE IN *VENICE* WE'D LOOK AT THE ACROPOLIS.

OH, REALLY? WE'D *CERTAINLY* BE FAMOUS THEN--FOR OUR AMAZING EYESIGHT, SINCE THE ACROPOLIS IS IN *GREECE*, YOU BIG--YOU BIG--!

OKAY, HERE IT FINALLY COMES. GET READY FOR THE *FAT* JOKES.

I KNEW IT WAS JUST A MATTER OF TIME BEFORE YOU SHOWED HOW *SHALLOW* A FRIEND YOU REALLY ARE. BACK WHEN I WAS LEADING-MAN HANDSOME--

YOU WERE STILL A BIG JERK *AND* A MEANYHEAD THEN TOO, BUT AT *LEAST* YOU WERE RATIONAL.

OKAY, MAYBE NOT RATIONAL BY ANY CIVILIZED STANDARD, BUT YOU HAD YOUR OWN TWISTED LOGIC AND GUTTER VIRTUES THAT WERE *ACTUALLY* PRETTY RELIABLE, ONCE I GOT TO KNOW YOU.

NOW LOOK AT YOU! YOU CAN *BARELY* HOLD YOURSELF UPRIGHT, BUT ALL OF A SUDDEN YOU ABSOLUTELY HAD TO GO TRUDGING UP THE SIDE OF A MOUNTAIN?

TELL ME HOW THAT MAKES *ANY* SENSE!

UH... WELL...UH... THE THING IS--

89

BACK WITH THAT OTHER FELLOW NAMED JACK...

HURRY!

HURRY!

PUSH *HARDER*, YOU SIMPERING LITTLE WORM!

THAT SORT OF TALK ISN'T *HELPING*, JACK!

THE CAVE ENTRANCE IS JUST ABOVE US! I CAN *FEEL* IT!

WE NEED TO MAKE IT TO THE CAVE!

WATCH THE TAIL, JACK!

WATCH THE TAIL!

AND WHY DO WE HAVE TO GET INTO A CAVE? WHAT'S GOING ON WITH YOU?

I DON'T *KNOW!*

DO YOU THINK I GROW A GODDAMN *CROCODILE* TAIL EVERY DAY?

NO FAT CHICKS

I DON'T THINK IT'S QUITE CROCODILIAN, JACK. IT'S GOT MORE OF AN IGUANA-ISH *LOOK* TO ME. OR MAYBE MORE LIKE ONE OF THOSE DESERT HORNY TOADS.

NEVER MIND! JUST GET ME TO THE CAVE, BEFORE--

--WELL, I DON'T KNOW *WHAT!* BUT GET ME THERE!

BACK IN THOSE OTHER CAVES (APPARENTLY IT'S ALL DONE IN CAVES NOW)...

FOR GENERATIONS OF OUR TRIBES THE SORCERERS OF THE EMPIRE RULED US, *CONTROLLING* US WITH THEIR MAGIC, FORCING US TO DO THEIR BIDDING.

BUT THEN, SUDDENLY ONE NIGHT, A SINGLE HAND-GRASP OF YEARS AGO, THEY ALL LEFT, AND WE WERE FREE AGAIN, FOR THE *FIRST* TIME IN UNMARKED CENTURIES.

FREE TO HUNT, TO STRIKE THE FARMS AND KEEPS OF THE SURFACE DWELLERS AS WE CHOSE TO, AND NOT JUST AT THE BIDDING OF OUR *HATED* MASTERS.

"EXCEPT THAT WE WERE MISTAKEN. ONE POWERFUL SORCERER REMAINED--OR RETURNED."

WAKUN SUL DOR ENIKAN! ERIKUDES SUL HERAK DA SULLOS SUL DOR KRAGUS OD DA TERUN HA!

"ONE MOON CYCLE PAST HE REACHED OUT WITH HIS SORCERIES AGAIN, SEEKING TO *BIND* US ONCE MORE. WE'VE BEEN RESISTING, BUT HIS MIGHT INCREASES NIGHT BY NIGHT."

ERSAKENUN UN ANDERU KRAGUS OD BUNDUN, UN MECKHAN BEHAL!

AND THAT'S HOW I RECEIVED MY SECOND HEROIC COMMISSION IN AS MANY NIGHTS.

WHAT'S YOUR NAME AGAIN?

BRAK PAK K'RAK. KILLER OF MANY FOES. BITER OF ENEMY SKULLS.

IN THE FIRST PLACE, I WAS STILL OBLIGATED, BY UNBREAKABLE HERO'S OATH, TO RESCUE ELSA FEN, HER FAMILY, AND THEIR RETAINERS, FROM THE MONSTERS.

BUT YOU CAN CALL ME BRAK FOR SHORT.

AND THE KING SENT YOU ALONG WITH ME TO MAKE SURE I WOULDN'T FORGET THE MISSION AND RUN OFF, TRYING TO SAVE MY OWN SKIN?

BUT IN ORDER TO DO THAT, I HAD TO SUCCEED AT MY SECOND QUEST, TO HELP THOSE SAME MONSTERS FREE THEMSELVES FROM A MIGHTY SORCERER.

PARTLY. BUT ALSO, ASSUMING YOU BRAVELY DO YOUR DUTY, I AM TO SACRIFICE MYSELF, FOR THE GOOD OF THE TRIBES.

HOW SO?

TO TEST THE CURRENT EXTENT OF THE SORCERER'S POWER. WHEN WE GET CLOSE ENOUGH TO HIS TOWER, I WILL FALL UNDER HIS SPELL, AND MOST LIKELY TRY TO KILL YOU, FORCING YOU TO KILL ME.

THEN YOU WILL KNOW FIRST CLAW WHAT DANGERS YOU FACE.

I WANTED AN ADVENTUROUS LIFE, AND I GOT IT.

AH, I SEE. YOU'RE THE GUINEA PIG. OR THE CANARY IN THE COAL MINE. OR THE JUDAS GOAT. THERE'S THIS ONE WORLD WITH SUCH LOVELY METAPHORS.

WE'RE HERE, JACK FROST. YONDER IS THE TOWER OF THE SORCERER.

99

OKAY, JACK, YOU FOUND YOUR *CAVE*.

JUST IN TIME, TOO!

JUST IN TIME FOR WHAT?

I'M NOT SURE. I THINK THERE'S GOING TO BE *ANOTHER* TRANSFORMATION. I THINK I'M GOING TO FINISH TURNING INTO WHATEVER I'M TURNING INTO.

WHICH, BY THE WAY, *PROVES* I WASN'T JUST GETTING FAT. THERE'S DEFINITELY SOME BIG-TIME MAGICAL HOODOO AT WORK HERE.

TRUE ENOUGH, BUT NOT GOOD MAGIC.

FIRST I NEED TO GET THIS BRIEFCASE *OPEN* AND--

WOW!

THERE'S SO MUCH!

MY HOARD!

OH, CRAP!

HERE COMES THE REST OF THE-- OH, GOLLY DAMN, THIS HURTS!

THIS *REALLY* HURTS BAD!

BOB "SMILEY" GORDICHUK MAY HAVE BECOME THE POET LAUREATE OF ANAMOOSE, NORTH DAKOTA ONLY AFTER ED SUSSMAN DISAPPEARED UNDER *MYSTERIOUS* CIRCUMSTANCES, TRUE.

BUT THAT'S NOT TO SAY HE ISN'T DESERVING OF THE POST.

WHY, HIS FIRST COLLECTION, *SOME PENS I HAVE ENCOUNTERED*, HELD THE NUMBER ONE SPOT ON THE BOOK RACK AT HANK'S HARDWARE FOR SIX *WEEKS* STRAIGHT!

EYEBROWS WERE RAISED, HOWEVER, WHEN HIS NEXT COLLECTION, *I HAVE NOTHING TO FEEL GUILTY ABOUT*, WAS PUBLISHED--

--FOLLOWED *QUICKLY* BY *I'M SURE ED SUSSMAN IS ALIVE AND WELL SOMEWHERE, PROBABLY.*

BUT IT WASN'T UNTIL THE RELEASE OF *THAT SMELL FROM UNDERNEATH MY BACK PORCH IS NOTHING TO BE CONCERNED ABOUT* THAT FOLKS IN ANAMOOSE STARTED TO WORRY.

SADLY, THE PUBLICATION OF *I HAVE A GUN AND I'M AFRAID I MIGHT HURT MYSELF AND OTHER POEMS* HAS BEEN POSTPONED INDEFINITELY.

"YOU, SIR, ARE **CLEARLY** A DICK."

Jack Dragon

❧ THE NEW ADVENTURES OF JACK AND JACK Part 4 of 4 ❧

BUT THAT LED TO ALSO WORKING FOR THOSE VERY MONSTERS TO REMOVE A MONSTER OF A DIFFERENT STRIPE PREYING ON *THEM.*

YOU'RE GOING TO DIE, YOU KNOW.

EXCUSE ME?

AND SOMEHOW BOTH QUESTS GOT TIED UP WITH EACH OTHER, SO THAT I BASICALLY HAVE TO SAVE EVERYONE IN THE FOREST FROM SOMETHING OR OTHER.

YOU'RE A *BRUTE.* AN ARMED THUG.

AND LET ME TELL YOU, IT'S A BIG FOREST.

WHEREAS *I* AM ONE OF THE MOST GIFTED PRACTITIONERS IN THE EMPIRE.

THIS SORCERER BETTER NOT TURN OUT TO ALSO BE IN NEED OF A HERO OF HIS OWN, OR I MIGHT JUST QUIT THE BUSINESS FOREVER.

DO YOU HONESTLY IMAGINE A SIMPLE KNIFE OR SWORD COULD *EVER* HARM ME? DO YOU THINK I'D ALLOW THAT?

BUT SO FAR HE SEEMS UNREPENTANTLY EVIL ENOUGH--GOD BLESS 'IM.

TRUTH IS, I HAD SOME HOPES ALONG THOSE LINES.

BUT I DO WANT TO POINT OUT THAT YOUR LOCALIZED EARTHQUAKE DIDN'T KILL ME, SO I GOT *THAT* GOING FOR ME.

SILLY CHILD.

THE EARTHQUAKE WASN'T THE ATTACK. *THAT* WAS MERELY A PRELUDE.

THE EARTHQUAKE WAS REQUIRED SIMPLY TO OPEN UP THE SUBTERRANEAN PASSAGES TO ALLOW MY *TRUE* ATTACK ACCESS TO THE SURFACE.

THE DEEP CRAWLERS!

THEY'RE DEDICATED MAN-EATERS, BY THE WAY.

YEAH, I SORT OF GUESSED AS MUCH.

ALL IN ALL, THIS ISN'T TURNING OUT SO WELL.

THEY PILE UP, CRAWLING OVER THE CARCASSES OF THEIR FALLEN IN ORDER TO GET TO ME.

AND AS TOUGH AS I AM, THEIR BITES STILL TAKE CHUNKS OF MY FLESH.

I'M GOING UNDER.

AT LEAST I WAS ABLE TO LIVE THE LAST FEW DAYS OF MY LIFE ON MY OWN TERMS-- DOING WHAT I'VE COME TO LOVE IN SUCH A SHORT TIME.

THAT'S GOT TO BE SOME COMFORT IN THE END, RIGHT?

THAT'S OKAY, BRAK.

WORRIED HE MIGHT FALL UNDER YOUR SWAY, BRAK WAS KIND ENOUGH TO TELL ME ABOUT HIS *GLASS* SNOUT.

NOW, BACK TO YOU, MAGICIAN.

YOUR VICTORY OVER MY THRALL WILL DO YOU NO GOOD, ADVENTURER. YOU'VE NO WEAPONS LEFT AND I'M STILL *FLUSHED* WITH EVERY SORT OF POWER.

POSSIBLY.

BUT THEN I'M CURIOUS WHY YOU HAVEN'T BLASTED ME WITH ANYTHING NEW.

I'M BEGINNING TO WONDER IF YOU HAVEN'T EXPENDED YOUR ENTIRE MENU OF READY SPELLS.

CAN YOU TAKE THAT RISK? MAYBE WE SHOULD TALK ABOUT--

AND DO YOU KNOW WHAT *ELSE* I WONDER?

NO. WHAT WOULD THAT BE?

ARE YOU FEELING OKAY NOW, BUDDY?

MUCH BETTER NOW, JACK OF THE FROST. IS THE SORCERER DEAD?

FOR HIS SAKE I HOPE SO. OTHERWISE THOSE BIG BUGS FEEDING ON ALL OF HIS SQUISHED *PARTS* HAS TO HURT LIKE THE DICKENS.

YOU WERE *QUITE* BRAVE IN THE FACE OF DIRE SORCERY, PINK ONE.

NOT AS MUCH AS YOU'D THINK. I WAS RAISED BY THE EMPIRE'S *TOP* SORCERESS AND SHE TAUGHT ME A LOT ABOUT THE COMMUNITY.

SHE DIDN'T HAVE MUCH RESPECT FOR RESEARCH TYPES WHO LEARNED A FEW NASTY SPELLS AND SUDDENLY *THOUGHT* THEY COULD MAKE IT AS A COMBAT SORCERER.

IT'S KIND OF A SPECIALIZED FIELD. IN ANY CASE, I HAD THIS ONE PEGGED AS AN AMATEUR COMBAT TYPE *RIGHT* AWAY.

YOU KNEW ALL ALONG YOU COULD BEAT HIM?

LET'S JUST SAY I WAS CONFIDENT. THOSE GIANT BUGS OF HIS GAVE ME A FEW TENSE MOMENTS, THOUGH.

HE NEARLY *GOT* ME WITH THE BUGS.

A DAY OR SO LATER...

AND BASICALLY, THAT WAS THAT.

LIFT YOUR STEINS AND GOBLETS, LADIES AND GENTLEMEN!

ANOTHER TOAST TO THE **HERO** OF THE DAY!

TO *MacDUFF!*

THE GRAND AND PUISSANT WISE BIRD WHO BROUGHT PEACE TO OUR LAND, AFTER SO MANY **YEARS** OF STRIFE AND TERROR!

TO *MacDUFF!*

TO *MacDUFF!*

SORRY, JACK. **YOU** SHOULD BE THE GUY GETTING TOASTED.

BUT THAT'S THE WAY OF THINGS, HUH? I DID MY PART IN FRONT OF A LOT OF WITNESSES, SO I GET THE CREDIT, WHILE YOU **BASICALLY** ACTED OFF STAGE AS FAR AS THEY'RE CONCERNED.

DON'T FRET, PARTNER. YOU DESERVE **THIS**. BEATING UP A BULLY IS ONE THING. FORGING A FAIR TREATY AMONG FORMER ENEMIES IS ANOTHER.

TAKE YOUR BOWS WITH MY BLESSING.

THERE YOU ARE, JACK FROST!

OH MY!

A HERO'S **RIGHTFUL** REWARD.

OH, GOOD, SO HE'S OF A LIKE MIND, THEN.

SUCH A GREAT **WEDDING** YOU TWO KIDS WILL HAVE!

UH...I'M SORRY, SIR... WHAT DID YOU JUST SAY?

OH, I MEANT TO MENTION THAT PART, JACK. THEY HAVE A CUSTOM THAT, WELL, WHEN YOU SAVE THE GIRL, YOU **GET** THE GIRL.

LONG STORY SHORT: MacDUFF AND I HIGHTAILED IT TO ANOTHER WORLD THE MOMENT THE POWER TO DO SO BUILT UP IN ME.

I'D MEET ELSA FEN AND BRAK THE MONSTER AGAIN, BUT THAT'S ANOTHER STORY.

THAT ISN'T TRUE. IF SOME OTHER GUY'S STUPID OLD STORY CAN TELL ME SOMETHING ABOUT MYSELF, THEN I'M INTERESTED IN THAT *TOO.*

BUT ONLY THE SHORT VERSION AND *ONLY* THE PARTS ABOUT ME.

"WELL, THE SHORT VERSION IS THIS. ONCE UPON A TIME THERE WAS THIS EVIL, GREEDY LITTLE TROLL WHO ONLY LIKED TWO THINGS-- GETTING RICH AND FORNICATING WITH WOMEN."

COME HERE, YOU LEGENDARY RHINE MAIDENS! I GOT SOME OF WHAT YOU *NEED!*

"SO ONE DAY HE KILLED HIS OWN FATHER TO GET HIS GOLD. BUT HE WAS SO GREEDY THAT HE WOULDN'T EVEN SHARE IT WITH HIS BROTHER."

NO WAY! THIS IS *ALL* MINE!

DAD'S GOLD

"THE TROLL HID HIMSELF AWAY, GUARDING HIS HOARD JEALOUSLY WHERE, OVER TIME, HIS GREED AND THE FACT THAT HE CARED MORE FOR HIS GOLD THAN FOR MANKIND SLOWLY TURNED HIM INTO A DRAGON."

I GUESS I CAN LIVE WITH THIS--AS LONG AS I GOT THE GOLD.

DAD'S GOLD